This igloo book belongs to:

....

igloobooks

Published in 2017
by Igloo Books Ltd
Cottage Farm
Sywell
NN6 0BJ
www.igloobooks.com

REX001 0317
2 4 6 8 10 9 7 5 3 1
ISBN 978-1-78670-447-4

Produced under license for

carte blanche

© 2016 Carte Blanche Greetings Limited ® cbg.co.uk
The Tiny Tatty Teddy Logo and the Me to You
oval are registered Trade Marks of Carte Blanche
Greetings Limited.

Designed by Elitsa Veshkova
Written by Claire Mowat

Printed and manufactured in China

igloobooks

Daddy, you're my hero, the greatest and the best.

You're more than just a daddy...

... and not like all the rest.

One day you'll be a plane, flying me high up in the sky.

Then you're a chef in the kitchen, baking a yummy pie.

If a toy gets broken, you can always make it go.

Daddy, there's nothing in the world that you don't know.

You're the greatest at building dens and houses in a tree.

At the seaside we dig huge sandcastles and sit by the sea.

We rush outside on windy days... ... to fly my big bright kite.

I'm careful not to let it float away...

... and hold the string quite tight.

You're the best footballer ever, but you always let me score.

However long we play for, there's always time for more.

I love our adventures in the garden, digging up the dirt.

You're always there to dry my tears whenever I get hurt.

You tell me silly jokes that are always very funny.

Tee-hee

Sometimes I laugh so hard, it really hurts my tummy.

At story time, you tuck me in and tell me not to wriggle.

I don't need a superhero like the ones on TV.

Daddy, you are my hero, the best there will ever be!